Yay!
You're engaged!

THIS DIARY BELONGS TO

....

IF FOUND PLEASE CALL

....

And so the
adventure
begins...

THEY LIKED IT, SO THEY

Put a ring on it!

Congratulations on your engagement!

This planner will be a safe place for all of your thoughts,
goals and general wedding planning business.

Set your budget, research vendors, track your guestlist and
organise your daily appointments all in one handy little book.
This planner is designed to suit all couples, if any of the infomation
included does not apply to you or your bridal party,
simply skip ahead to the next point.

Let's get started on organising your dream wedding!

ABOUT YOU

Your name & age:

....

....

Where do you live?

....

....

What is your occupation?

....

....

What are your hobbies?

....

....

....

What is your favourite thing to do on
a Saturday night?

....

....

....

....

What are you looking forward to
most about your wedding day?

....

....

....

....

....

Fiancé's name & age:

....

....

Where do you live?

....

....

What is your occupation?

....

....

What are your hobbies?

....

....

....

What is your favourite thing to do on
a Saturday night?

....

....

....

....

What are you looking forward to
most about your wedding day?

....

....

....

....

....

THE PROPOSAL

No doubt you have re told this story a million times by now, but even so, you might forget the details in years to come.

What was your proposal date? ....

Where did all this take place? ....

....

Details

....
....
....
....
....
....
....
....
....
....
....
....
....
....
....
....
....
....
....
....

PLAN OF ATTACK

Ok, so you're engaged, you've celebrated, now what?
Use this check list throughout the year to keep track of what to do and when.

12 MONTHS OUT

If you have your heart set on a celebrant, photographer or band book them in PRONTO!

- [ ] Set a wedding date
- [ ] Set a budget
- [ ] Compile a rough guest list
- [ ] Book ceremony & reception venues
- [ ] Book your celebrant, priest or minister
- [ ] Book a photographer
- [ ] Choose bridal party (don't rush this decision!)
- [ ] Start considering your wedding theme (beach, boho, vintage, classic, rustic, elegant, relaxed... use your imagination)
- [ ] Decide on a colour scheme
- [ ] Get excited!

9-11 MONTHS OUT

- [ ] Start shopping for your outfits
- [ ] Book honeymoon
- [ ] Select a gift registry (if having one)

- [ ] Book caterer
- [ ] Shop for bridal party outfits
- [ ] Book cars
- [ ] Choose rings
- [ ] Order wedding cake
- [ ] Book florist
- [ ] Book band/DJ/entertainment

6 MONTHS OUT

- [ ] Choose dates for hens and/or bucks parties
- [ ] Order invitations and stationery
- [ ] Finalise guest list
- [ ] Collect postal addresses for invitations
- [ ] Meet with celebrant to discuss service
- [ ] Book accommodation for the wedding night
- [ ] Update passports if necessary
- [ ] Have hair trial
- [ ] Have make up trial
- [ ] Schedule dance lessons
- [ ] Arrange bonbonniere
- [ ] Meet with photographer

Tip!

Organise food for your bridal party to have while getting ready.

- [ ] Request annual leave for honeymoon
- [ ] Purchase bridal party gifts
- [ ] Choose ceremony and reception music
- [ ] Discuss final plans with florist

3 MONTHS OUT

- [ ] Send invitations
- [ ] Book final fittings
- [ ] Purchase lingerie/underwear
- [ ] Choose an MC
- [ ] Purchase a guest book
- [ ] Order wedding programs
- [ ] Complete notice of intended marriage (celebrant will help with this)
- [ ] Order place cards and any signage

1 MONTH CHECKLIST

- [ ] Collect RSVPs
- [ ] Arrange seating plans
- [ ] Have engagement ring cleaned

- [ ] Pick up wedding outfits
- [ ] Write your vows
- [ ] Write speeches and toasts
- [ ] Break in your wedding shoes
- [ ] Create running order sheets for the day and give to designated people (including important phone numbers and vendor information)

LAST WEEK CHECKLIST

- [ ] Clean your house
- [ ] Have hair coloured and/or cut
- [ ] Get manicure, pedicure, tan, etc.
- [ ] Give venue final head count
- [ ] Pick up rings
- [ ] Drop off decorations to venues
- [ ] Attend rehearsal
- [ ] Pack for honeymoon
- [ ] Relax, everything's done!

NOTES

Weekly Planner

I will love
you.
Today.
tomorrow.
always

IMPORTANT DATES

JANUARY	FEBRUARY	MARCH

APRIL	MAY	JUNE

JULY	AUGUST	SEPTEMBER

OCTOBER	NOVEMBER	DECEMBER

Week of

MONDAY	TUESDAY	WEDNESDAY	THURSDAY

PERSONAL TO DO LIST:

....
....
....
....
....
....

WEDDING TO DO LIST:

....
....
....
....
....
....

FRIDAY	SATURDAY	SUNDAY

....
....
....
....
....
....
....
....
....
....
....
....
....
....
....
....
....

NOTES:

....
....
....
....
....
....

Week of

MONDAY	TUESDAY	WEDNESDAY	THURSDAY

PERSONAL TO DO LIST:

WEDDING TO DO LIST:

FRIDAY	SATURDAY	SUNDAY

....
....
....
....
....
....
....
....
....
....
....
....
....
....
....
....
....
....

NOTES:

....
....
....
....
....
....
....

Week of

MONDAY	TUESDAY	WEDNESDAY	THURSDAY

PERSONAL TO DO LIST:

WEDDING TO DO LIST:

FRIDAY	SATURDAY	SUNDAY

THIS WEEK'S FOCUS:

....
....
....
....
....
....
....
....
....
....
....
....
....
....
....
....
....
....
....

NOTES:

....
....
....
....
....
....

Week of

MONDAY	TUESDAY	WEDNESDAY	THURSDAY

PERSONAL TO DO LIST:

....

....

....

....

....

....

WEDDING TO DO LIST:

....

....

....

....

....

....

FRIDAY	SATURDAY	SUNDAY

THIS
WEEK'S
FOCUS:

· ·
· ·
· ·
· ·
· ·
· ·
· ·
· ·
· ·
· ·
· ·
· ·
· ·
· ·
· ·
· ·

NOTES:

· ·
· ·
· ·
· ·
· ·

Week of

MONDAY	TUESDAY	WEDNESDAY	THURSDAY

PERSONAL TO DO LIST:

WEDDING TO DO LIST:

FRIDAY	SATURDAY	SUNDAY

....
....
....
....
....
....
....
....
....
....
....
....
....
....
....
....
....
....

NOTES:

....
....
....
....
....
....

Week of

MONDAY	TUESDAY	WEDNESDAY	THURSDAY

PERSONAL TO DO LIST:

WEDDING TO DO LIST:

FRIDAY	SATURDAY	SUNDAY

....
....
....
....
....
....
....
....
....
....
....
....
....
....
....
....
....
....
....
....

NOTES:

....
....
....
....
....
....

Week of

MONDAY	TUESDAY	WEDNESDAY	THURSDAY

PERSONAL TO DO LIST:

WEDDING TO DO LIST:

FRIDAY	SATURDAY	SUNDAY

THIS WEEK'S FOCUS:

....
....
....
....
....
....
....
....
....
....
....
....
....
....
....
....
....
....
....
....

NOTES:

....
....
....
....
....
....

Week of

MONDAY	TUESDAY	WEDNESDAY	THURSDAY

PERSONAL TO DO LIST:

WEDDING TO DO LIST:

FRIDAY	SATURDAY	SUNDAY

THIS WEEK'S FOCUS:

....
....
....
....
....
....
....
....
....
....
....
....
....
....
....
....
....

NOTES:

....
....
....
....
....
....
....

Week of

MONDAY	TUESDAY	WEDNESDAY	THURSDAY

PERSONAL TO DO LIST:

....
....
....
....
....
....

WEDDING TO DO LIST:

....
....
....
....
....
....

FRIDAY	SATURDAY	SUNDAY

THIS WEEK'S FOCUS:

....
....
....
....
....
....
....
....
....
....
....
....
....
....
....
....
....

NOTES:

....
....
....
....
....
....

Week of

MONDAY	TUESDAY	WEDNESDAY	THURSDAY

PERSONAL TO DO LIST:

WEDDING TO DO LIST:

FRIDAY	SATURDAY	SUNDAY

THIS WEEK'S FOCUS:

....
....
....
....
....
....
....
....
....
....
....
....
....
....
....
....
....
....
....

NOTES:

....
....
....
....
....
....

Week of

MONDAY	TUESDAY	WEDNESDAY	THURSDAY

PERSONAL TO DO LIST:

....

....

....

....

....

....

WEDDING TO DO LIST:

....

....

....

....

....

....

FRIDAY	SATURDAY	SUNDAY

NOTES:

Week of

MONDAY	TUESDAY	WEDNESDAY	THURSDAY

PERSONAL TO DO LIST:

WEDDING TO DO LIST:

FRIDAY	SATURDAY	SUNDAY

THIS WEEK'S FOCUS:

....
....
....
....
....
....
....
....
....
....
....
....
....
....
....
....
....
....

NOTES:

....
....
....
....
....
....

Week of

MONDAY	TUESDAY	WEDNESDAY	THURSDAY

PERSONAL TO DO LIST:

....
....
....
....
....
....

WEDDING TO DO LIST:

....
....
....
....
....
....

FRIDAY	SATURDAY	SUNDAY

THIS WEEK'S FOCUS:

....
....
....
....
....
....
....
....
....
....
....
....
....
....
....
....
....
....
....

NOTES:

....
....
....
....
....
....

Week of

MONDAY	TUESDAY	WEDNESDAY	THURSDAY

PERSONAL TO DO LIST:

....
....
....
....
....
....

WEDDING TO DO LIST:

....
....
....
....
....
....

FRIDAY	SATURDAY	SUNDAY

....
....
....
....
....
....
....
....
....
....
....
....
....
....
....
....
....
....

NOTES:

....
....
....
....
....
....

Week of

MONDAY	TUESDAY	WEDNESDAY	THURSDAY

PERSONAL TO DO LIST:

WEDDING TO DO LIST:

FRIDAY	SATURDAY	SUNDAY

....
....
....
....
....
....
....
....
....
....
....
....
....
....
....
....
....
....

NOTES:

....
....
....
....
....
....
....

Week of

MONDAY	TUESDAY	WEDNESDAY	THURSDAY

PERSONAL TO DO LIST:

....
....
....
....
....
....

WEDDING TO DO LIST:

....
....
....
....
....
....

FRIDAY	SATURDAY	SUNDAY

NOTES:

Week of

MONDAY	TUESDAY	WEDNESDAY	THURSDAY

PERSONAL TO DO LIST:

WEDDING TO DO LIST:

FRIDAY	SATURDAY	SUNDAY

THIS WEEK'S FOCUS:

....
....
....
....
....
....
....
....
....
....
....
....
....
....
....
....
....
....

NOTES:

....
....
....
....
....
....

Week of

MONDAY	TUESDAY	WEDNESDAY	THURSDAY

PERSONAL TO DO LIST:

WEDDING TO DO LIST:

FRIDAY	SATURDAY	SUNDAY

THIS WEEK'S FOCUS:

....
....
....
....
....
....
....
....
....
....
....
....
....
....
....
....
....
....
....

NOTES:

....
....
....
....
....
....

Week of

MONDAY	TUESDAY	WEDNESDAY	THURSDAY

PERSONAL TO DO LIST:

WEDDING TO DO LIST:

FRIDAY	SATURDAY	SUNDAY

THIS
WEEK'S
FOCUS:

....
....
....
....
....
....
....
....
....
....
....
....
....
....
....
....
....
....

NOTES:

....
....
....
....
....
....

Week of

MONDAY	TUESDAY	WEDNESDAY	THURSDAY

PERSONAL TO DO LIST:

....
....
....
....
....
....

WEDDING TO DO LIST:

....
....
....
....
....
....

FRIDAY	SATURDAY	SUNDAY

THIS WEEK'S FOCUS:

....
....
....
....
....
....
....
....
....
....
....
....
....
....
....
....
....
....

NOTES:

....
....
....
....
....
....
....

Week of

MONDAY	TUESDAY	WEDNESDAY	THURSDAY

PERSONAL TO DO LIST:

WEDDING TO DO LIST:

FRIDAY	SATURDAY	SUNDAY

THIS WEEK'S FOCUS:

....
....
....
....
....
....
....
....
....
....
....
....
....
....
....
....
....
....

NOTES:

....
....
....
....
....
....

Week of

MONDAY	TUESDAY	WEDNESDAY	THURSDAY

PERSONAL TO DO LIST:

WEDDING TO DO LIST:

FRIDAY	SATURDAY	SUNDAY

....
....
....
....
....
....
....
....
....
....
....
....
....
....
....
....
....
....
....

NOTES:

....
....
....
....
....
....

Week of

MONDAY	TUESDAY	WEDNESDAY	THURSDAY

PERSONAL TO DO LIST:

WEDDING TO DO LIST:

FRIDAY	SATURDAY	SUNDAY

....
....
....
....
....
....
....
....
....
....
....
....
....
....
....
....
....

NOTES:

....
....
....
....
....
....

Week of

MONDAY	TUESDAY	WEDNESDAY	THURSDAY

PERSONAL TO DO LIST:

WEDDING TO DO LIST:

FRIDAY	SATURDAY	SUNDAY

THIS
WEEK'S
FOCUS:

....

....

....

....

....

....

....

....

....

....

....

....

....

....

....

....

....

....

....

NOTES:

....

....

....

....

....

....

Week of

MONDAY	TUESDAY	WEDNESDAY	THURSDAY

PERSONAL TO DO LIST:

WEDDING TO DO LIST:

FRIDAY	SATURDAY	SUNDAY

....
....
....
....
....
....
....
....
....
....
....
....
....
....
....
....
....
....

NOTES:

....
....
....
....
....
....

Week of

MONDAY	TUESDAY	WEDNESDAY	THURSDAY

PERSONAL TO DO LIST:

WEDDING TO DO LIST:

FRIDAY	SATURDAY	SUNDAY	THIS WEEK'S FOCUS:
			....
			....
			....
			....
			....
			....
			....
			....
			....
			....
			....
			....
			....
			....
			....
			....
			....

NOTES:

....
....
....
....
....
....

Week of

MONDAY	TUESDAY	WEDNESDAY	THURSDAY

PERSONAL TO DO LIST:

WEDDING TO DO LIST:

FRIDAY	SATURDAY	SUNDAY	THIS WEEK'S FOCUS:

NOTES:

Week of

MONDAY	TUESDAY	WEDNESDAY	THURSDAY

PERSONAL TO DO LIST:

....
....
....
....
....
....

WEDDING TO DO LIST:

....
....
....
....
....
....

FRIDAY	SATURDAY	SUNDAY

THIS WEEK'S FOCUS:

....

....

....

....

....

....

....

....

....

....

....

....

....

....

....

....

....

....

....

NOTES:

....

....

....

....

....

....

Week of

MONDAY	TUESDAY	WEDNESDAY	THURSDAY

PERSONAL TO DO LIST:

....

....

....

....

....

....

WEDDING TO DO LIST:

....

....

....

....

....

....

FRIDAY	SATURDAY	SUNDAY

THIS
WEEK'S
FOCUS:

....
....
....
....
....
....
....
....
....
....
....
....
....
....
....
....
....
....

NOTES:

....
....
....
....
....
....

Week of

MONDAY	TUESDAY	WEDNESDAY	THURSDAY

PERSONAL TO DO LIST:

....

....

....

....

....

....

WEDDING TO DO LIST:

....

....

....

....

....

....

FRIDAY	SATURDAY	SUNDAY

THIS
WEEK'S
FOCUS:

NOTES:

Week of

MONDAY	TUESDAY	WEDNESDAY	THURSDAY

PERSONAL TO DO LIST:

WEDDING TO DO LIST:

FRIDAY	SATURDAY	SUNDAY

THIS
WEEK'S
FOCUS:

....
....
....
....
....
....
....
....
....
....
....
....
....
....
....
....
....
....

NOTES:

....
....
....
....
....
....

Week of

MONDAY	TUESDAY	WEDNESDAY	THURSDAY

PERSONAL TO DO LIST:

....
....
....
....
....
....

WEDDING TO DO LIST:

....
....
....
....
....
....

FRIDAY	SATURDAY	SUNDAY

THIS
WEEK'S
FOCUS:

NOTES:

Week of

MONDAY	TUESDAY	WEDNESDAY	THURSDAY

PERSONAL TO DO LIST:

WEDDING TO DO LIST:

FRIDAY	SATURDAY	SUNDAY

....
....
....
....
....
....
....
....
....
....
....
....
....
....
....
....
....
....

NOTES:

....
....
....
....
....
....

Week of

MONDAY	TUESDAY	WEDNESDAY	THURSDAY

PERSONAL TO DO LIST:

WEDDING TO DO LIST:

FRIDAY	SATURDAY	SUNDAY

THIS
WEEK'S
FOCUS:

....

....

....

....

....

....

....

....

....

....

....

....

....

....

....

....

....

....

NOTES:

....

....

....

....

....

Week of

MONDAY	TUESDAY	WEDNESDAY	THURSDAY

PERSONAL TO DO LIST:

WEDDING TO DO LIST:

FRIDAY	SATURDAY	SUNDAY

THIS WEEK'S FOCUS:

....

....

....

....

....

....

....

....

....

....

....

....

....

....

....

....

NOTES:

....

....

....

....

....

....

Week of

MONDAY	TUESDAY	WEDNESDAY	THURSDAY

PERSONAL TO DO LIST:

....

....

....

....

....

....

WEDDING TO DO LIST:

....

....

....

....

....

....

FRIDAY	SATURDAY	SUNDAY

....
....
....
....
....
....
....
....
....
....
....
....
....
....
....
....
....
....

NOTES:

....
....
....
....
....
....

Week of

MONDAY	TUESDAY	WEDNESDAY	THURSDAY

PERSONAL TO DO LIST:

WEDDING TO DO LIST:

FRIDAY	SATURDAY	SUNDAY

THIS
WEEK'S
FOCUS:

....
....
....
....
....
....
....
....
....
....
....
....
....
....
....
....
....
....

NOTES:

....
....
....
....
....
....
....

Week of

MONDAY	TUESDAY	WEDNESDAY	THURSDAY

PERSONAL TO DO LIST:

WEDDING TO DO LIST:

FRIDAY	SATURDAY	SUNDAY

NOTES:

Week of

MONDAY	TUESDAY	WEDNESDAY	THURSDAY

PERSONAL TO DO LIST:

WEDDING TO DO LIST:

FRIDAY	SATURDAY	SUNDAY

....
....
....
....
....
....
....
....
....
....
....
....
....
....
....
....
....
....
....

NOTES:

....
....
....
....
....
....

Week of

MONDAY	TUESDAY	WEDNESDAY	THURSDAY

PERSONAL TO DO LIST:

....
....
....
....
....
....

WEDDING TO DO LIST:

....
....
....
....
....
....

FRIDAY	SATURDAY	SUNDAY

....
....
....
....
....
....
....
....
....
....
....
....
....
....
....
....
....

NOTES:

....
....
....
....
....
....

Week of

MONDAY	TUESDAY	WEDNESDAY	THURSDAY

PERSONAL TO DO LIST:

....

....

....

....

....

....

WEDDING TO DO LIST:

....

....

....

....

....

....

FRIDAY	SATURDAY	SUNDAY

THIS
WEEK'S
FOCUS:

....
....
....
....
....
....
....
....
....
....
....
....
....
....
....
....
....
....

NOTES:

....
....
....
....
....
....

Week of

MONDAY	TUESDAY	WEDNESDAY	THURSDAY

PERSONAL TO DO LIST:

WEDDING TO DO LIST:

FRIDAY	SATURDAY	SUNDAY

THIS WEEK'S FOCUS:

....
....
....
....
....
....
....
....
....
....
....
....
....
....
....
....
....
....
....

NOTES:

....
....
....
....
....
....

Week of

MONDAY	TUESDAY	WEDNESDAY	THURSDAY

PERSONAL TO DO LIST:

....

....

....

....

....

....

WEDDING TO DO LIST:

....

....

....

....

....

....

FRIDAY	SATURDAY	SUNDAY

THIS
WEEK'S
FOCUS:

....
....
....
....
....
....
....
....
....
....
....
....
....
....
....
....
....

NOTES:

....
....
....
....
....
....

Week of

MONDAY	TUESDAY	WEDNESDAY	THURSDAY

PERSONAL TO DO LIST:

WEDDING TO DO LIST:

FRIDAY	SATURDAY	SUNDAY

THIS WEEK'S FOCUS:

....
....
....
....
....
....
....
....
....
....
....
....
....
....
....
....

NOTES:

....
....
....
....
....
....

Week of

MONDAY	TUESDAY	WEDNESDAY	THURSDAY

PERSONAL TO DO LIST:

....

....

....

....

....

....

WEDDING TO DO LIST:

....

....

....

....

....

....

FRIDAY	SATURDAY	SUNDAY

THIS WEEK'S FOCUS:

....
....
....
....
....
....
....
....
....
....
....
....
....
....
....
....
....
....

NOTES:

....
....
....
....
....
....

Week of

MONDAY	TUESDAY	WEDNESDAY	THURSDAY

PERSONAL TO DO LIST:

....
....
....
....
....
....

WEDDING TO DO LIST:

....
....
....
....
....
....

FRIDAY	SATURDAY	SUNDAY

THIS
WEEK'S
FOCUS:

....
....
....
....
....
....
....
....
....
....
....
....
....
....
....
....
....
....

NOTES:

....
....
....
....
....
....
....

Week of

MONDAY	TUESDAY	WEDNESDAY	THURSDAY

PERSONAL TO DO LIST:

WEDDING TO DO LIST:

FRIDAY	SATURDAY	SUNDAY

THIS
WEEK'S
FOCUS:

....
....
....
....
....
....
....
....
....
....
....
....
....
....
....
....
....
....
....

NOTES:

....
....
....
....
....
....

Week of

MONDAY	TUESDAY	WEDNESDAY	THURSDAY

PERSONAL TO DO LIST:

....

....

....

....

....

....

WEDDING TO DO LIST:

....

....

....

....

....

....

FRIDAY	SATURDAY	SUNDAY

THIS WEEK'S FOCUS:

....
....
....
....
....
....
....
....
....
....
....
....
....
....
....
....
....
....
....
....
....

NOTES:

....
....
....
....
....
....

Week of

MONDAY	TUESDAY	WEDNESDAY	THURSDAY

PERSONAL TO DO LIST:

....

....

....

....

....

....

WEDDING TO DO LIST:

....

....

....

....

....

....

FRIDAY	SATURDAY	SUNDAY

NOTES:

Week of

MONDAY	TUESDAY	WEDNESDAY	THURSDAY

PERSONAL TO DO LIST:

WEDDING TO DO LIST:

FRIDAY	SATURDAY	SUNDAY

....
....
....
....
....
....
....
....
....
....
....
....
....
....
....
....
....

NOTES:

....
....
....
....
....
....
....

Week of

MONDAY	TUESDAY	WEDNESDAY	THURSDAY

PERSONAL TO DO LIST:

WEDDING TO DO LIST:

FRIDAY	SATURDAY	SUNDAY

NOTES:

Week of

MONDAY	TUESDAY	WEDNESDAY	THURSDAY

PERSONAL TO DO LIST:

....
....
....
....
....
....

WEDDING TO DO LIST:

....
....
....
....
....
....

FRIDAY	SATURDAY	SUNDAY

THIS WEEK'S FOCUS:

....

....

....

....

....

....

....

....

....

....

....

....

....

....

....

....

....

....

....

NOTES:

....

....

....

....

....

....

YEARLY REVIEW

What was the most memorable moment of this year?

....

....

....

....

What are your biggest accomplishments for this past year?

....

....

....

....

What are the biggest take aways from the past year?

....

....

....

....

What do you plan on doing differently next year?

....

....

....

....

What or who are you particularly grateful for this past year?

....

....

....

....

Budget

BUDGET

Your idea of a budget:

Your Fiancé's idea of a budget:

....

OK, so how are you paying for it?

....

....

How much can you contribute?

....

Other contributions:

....

....

How much can you save per week? ....

How long will it take to save? ....

How many people are on your rough guestlist? ....

Your "must haves":

....

....

Your Fiancé's "must haves":

....

....

Notes:

....

....

....

Using the information above, your rough guest countand the wedding budget summary, you can now set an amount that you are both comfortable with.

Your wedding budget is: ....

WEDDING BUDGET SUMMARY

EXPENSES	ALLOCATION %	ALLOCATED BUDGET	ESTIMATED COSTS	ACTUAL COSTS
CEREMONY	Suggested 20%			
RECEPTION	Suggested 35%			
PHOTOGRAPHY & VIDEOGRAPHY	Suggested 10%			
FLOWERS & DECORATIONS	Suggested 10%			
ENTERTAINMENT	Suggested 10%			
TRANSPORT	Suggested 5%			
FASHION	Suggested 2%			
STATIONERY & SIGNAGE	Suggested 2%			
BEAUTY	Suggested 2%			
GIFTS	Suggested 2%			
OTHER	Suggested 2%			
TOTAL	100%			

WEDDING BUDGET TRACKER

ITEM	QUOTED	DEPOSIT PAID	BALANCE DUE
CEREMONY			
CELEBRANT/PRIEST/MINISTER FEE			
LOCATION FEE			
EQUIPMENT HIRE (CHAIRS, UMBRELLAS ETC)			
MUSIC			
RECEPTION			
VENUE FEE			
CATERING			
DRINKS			
WEDDING CAKE			
DÉCOR			
RENTED ITEMS (LINEN, CHAIRS, LIGHTING, FLOORING, HEATING, DANCE FLOOR, ETC)			
PHOTOGRAPHY & VIDEOGRAPHY			
PHOTOGRAPHY			
VIDEOGRAPHY			
PHOTOBOOTH			

DUE DATE	VENDOR	CONTACT

WEDDING BUDGET TRACKER

ITEM	QUOTED	DEPOSIT PAID	BALANCE DUE
FLOWERS & DECORATIONS			
BOUQUET FOR BRIDE/S			
BUTTONHOLE FOR GROOM/S			
HAIRPIECES			
BOUQUET FOR BRIDAL PARTY			
BOUQUET TO TOSS			
FLOWERGIRL			
PAGE BOY			
PARENTS OF BRIDE/GROOM			
PARENTS OF GROOM/BRIDE			
CAKE FLOWERS			
CAKE STAND			
ARBOUR			
VASES			
CANDLES			
DECORATIONS			
ENTERTAINMENT			
CEREMONY MUSIC			
RECEPTION MUSIC			

DUE DATE	VENDOR	CONTACT

WEDDING BUDGET TRACKER

ITEM	QUOTED	DEPOSIT PAID	BALANCE DUE
TRANSPORT			
CAR/LIMO HIRE			
TAXI			
GUEST TRANSPORT/BUS			
PARKING			
FASHION			
DRESS/SUIT			
DRESS/SUIT			
ALTERATIONS			
VEIL			
TIES			
POCKET SQUARES			
SHOES			
SHOES			
ACCESSORIES (JEWELLERY, HAIR PIECES, CUFFLINKS ETC)			
BRIDAL PARTY OUTFITS			
BRIDAL PARTY SHOES			
FLOWERGIRL			
PAGE BOY			
RINGS			

DUE DATE	VENDOR	CONTACT

WEDDING BUDGET TRACKER

ITEM	QUOTED	DEPOSIT PAID	BALANCE DUE
STATIONERY & SIGNAGE			
SAVE-THE-DATE CARDS			
INVITATIONS AND RSVPS			
PROGRAMS			
SEATING AND PLACE CARDS			
MENU CARDS			
THANK-YOU CARDS			
POSTAGE			
WELCOME SIGN			
GUEST BOOK			
ENVELOPES			
BEAUTY			
HAIR			
MAKE UP			
BRIDAL PARTY HAIR			
BRIDAL PARTY MAKE UP			
TAN			
WAXING			
NAILS			
SHAVE			

DUE DATE	VENDOR	CONTACT

WEDDING BUDGET TRACKER

ITEM	QUOTED	DEPOSIT PAID	BALANCE DUE
GIFTS			
FOR EACH OTHER			
FOR BRIDAL PARTY			
FOR PARENTS			
FOR GUESTS (FAVOURS)			
FLOWERGIRL			
PAGE BOY			
MC			
OTHER			
BABYSITTER			
LAWN GAMES			
KIDS ENTERTAINMENT			
ACCOMODATION (NIGHT BEFORE)			
ACCOMODATION (ON WEDDING NIGHT)			
HENS/BUCKS PARTIES			
HONEYMOON			

DUE DATE	VENDOR	CONTACT

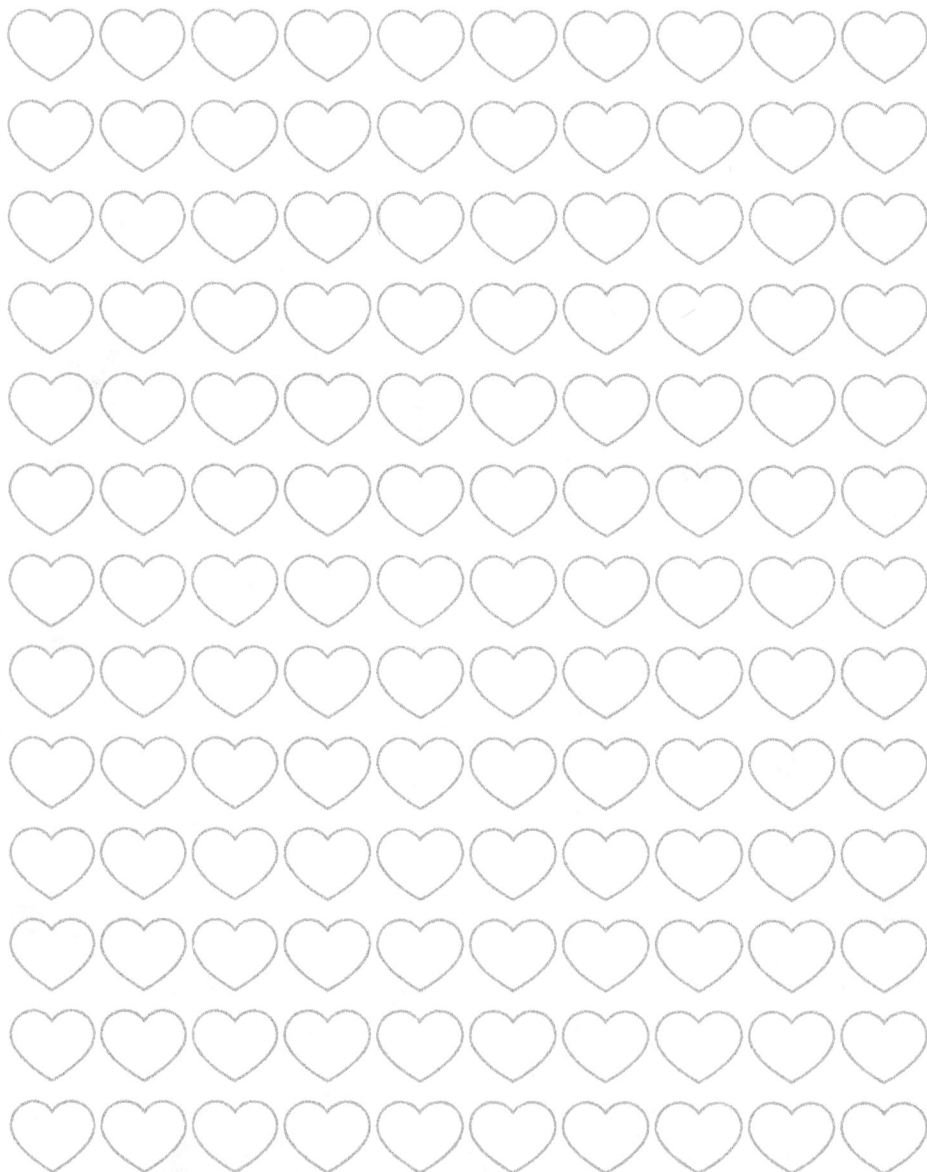

SAVINGS TRACKER

FUND:	EACH HEART EQUALS:	GOAL:

Vendors

VENDOR RESEARCH

VENUE

Quoted price ....
Phone ....
Email ....
Notes ....
....
....
....

PHOTOGRAPHY

Quoted price ....
Phone ....
Email ....
Notes ....
....
....
....

VENUE

Quoted price ....
Phone ....
Email ....
Notes ....
....
....
....

PHOTOGRAPHY

Quoted price ....
Phone ....
Email ....
Notes ....
....
....
....

VENUE

Quoted price ....
Phone ....
Email ....
Notes ....
....
....
....

PHOTOGRAPHY

Quoted price ....
Phone ....
Email ....
Notes ....
....
....
....

VIDEOGRAPHER

Quoted price ....

Phone ....

Email ....

Notes ....

....

....

....

CELEBRANT/PRIEST/MINISTER

Quoted price ....

Phone ....

Email ....

Notes ....

....

....

....

VIDEOGRAPHER

Quoted price ....

Phone ....

Email ....

Notes ....

....

....

....

CELEBRANT/PRIEST/MINISTER

Quoted price ....

Phone ....

Email ....

Notes ....

....

....

....

VIDEOGRAPHER

Quoted price ....

Phone ....

Email ....

Notes ....

....

....

....

CELEBRANT/PRIEST/MINISTER

Quoted price ....

Phone ....

Email ....

Notes ....

....

....

....

VENDOR RESEARCH

MUSIC

Quoted price ....
Phone ....
Email ....
Notes ....

....
....
....

ATTIRE

Quoted price ....
Phone ....
Email ....
Notes ....

....
....
....

MUSIC

Quoted price ....
Phone ....
Email ....
Notes ....

....
....
....

ATTIRE

Quoted price ....
Phone ....
Email ....
Notes ....

....
....
....

MUSIC

Quoted price ....
Phone ....
Email ....
Notes ....

....
....
....

ATTIRE

Quoted price ....
Phone ....
Email ....
Notes ....

....
....
....

CATERING

Quoted price ....

Phone ....

Email ....

Notes ....

....

....

....

TRANSPORT

Quoted price ....

Phone ....

Email ....

Notes ....

....

....

....

CATERING

Quoted price ....

Phone ....

Email ....

Notes ....

....

....

....

TRANSPORT

Quoted price ....

Phone ....

Email ....

Notes ....

....

....

....

CATERING

Quoted price ....

Phone ....

Email ....

Notes ....

....

....

....

TRANSPORT

Quoted price ....

Phone ....

Email ....

Notes ....

....

....

....

VENDOR RESEARCH

STATIONERY

Quoted price ....
Phone ....
Email ....
Notes ....
....
....
....

FLOWERS

Quoted price ....
Phone ....
Email ....
Notes ....
....
....
....

STATIONERY

Quoted price ....
Phone ....
Email ....
Notes ....
....
....
....

FLOWERS

Quoted price ....
Phone ....
Email ....
Notes ....
....
....
....

STATIONERY

Quoted price ....
Phone ....
Email ....
Notes ....
....
....
....

FLOWERS

Quoted price ....
Phone ....
Email ....
Notes ....
....
....
....

HONEYMOON

Quoted price

Phone

Email

Notes

OTHER

Quoted price

Phone

Email

Notes

HONEYMOON

Quoted price

Phone

Email

Notes

OTHER

Quoted price

Phone

Email

Notes

HONEYMOON

Quoted price

Phone

Email

Notes

OTHER

Quoted price

Phone

Email

Notes

VENUE RESEARCH

VENUE: ....

START & FINISH TIMES: ....

CONTACT: ....

SET UP & PACK DOWN TIMES: ....

PHONE/EMAIL: ....

DECOR RULES: (CONFETTI/CANDLES)
....

DATES AVAILABLE: ....

PARKING: ....

GUEST CAPACITY: ....

Is ours the only wedding that day?	Y	N
Is there an on the day coordinator?	Y	N
Are bathroom facilities available?	Y	N
Wheelchair and elderly accessible?	Y	N
Inhouse catering?	Y	N

VENUE PRICES

VENUE HIRE: ....

OTHER: ....

FOOD (PP): ....

ALCOHOL (PP): ....

NON-ALCOHOL (PP): ....

OTHER: ....

CHILD (PP): ....

CORKAGE IF BYO: ....

CAKE FEE: ....

OTHER: ....

CHAIRS & TABLES: ....

LINENS: ....

CROCKERY & GLASSWARE: ....

OTHER: ....

INCLEMENT WEATHER PLAN:

....

....

....

....

....

CANCELLATION POLICY:

....

....

....

....

....

VENUE FIT

RATE EVERYTHING OUT OF 5

LOCATION: ☆☆☆☆☆   TIME AVAILABLE: ☆☆☆☆☆

OVERALL PRICE: ☆☆☆☆☆   FOOD OPTIONS: ☆☆☆☆☆

STAFF: ☆☆☆☆☆   DRINK OPTIONS: ☆☆☆☆☆

DECOR: ☆☆☆☆☆   VIBE: ☆☆☆☆☆

DATES AVAILABLE: ☆☆☆☆☆

NOTES:

....

....

....

....

....

VENUE RESEARCH

VENUE: ....

CONTACT: ....

PHONE/EMAIL: ....

DATES AVAILABLE: ....

GUEST CAPACITY: ....

START & FINISH TIMES: ....

SET UP & PACK DOWN TIMES: ....

DECOR RULES: (CONFETTI/CANDLES)
....

PARKING: ....

	Y	N
Is ours the only wedding that day?	Y	N
Is there an on the day coordinator?	Y	N
Are bathroom facilities available?	Y	N
Wheelchair and elderly accessible?	Y	N
Inhouse catering?	Y	N

VENUE PRICES

VENUE HIRE: ....

FOOD (PP): ....

ALCOHOL (PP): ....

NON-ALCOHOL (PP): ....

CHILD (PP): ....

CORKAGE IF BYO: ....

CAKE FEE: ....

CHAIRS & TABLES: ....

LINENS: ....

CROCKERY & GLASSWARE: ....

OTHER: ....
....

OTHER: ....
....

OTHER: ....
....

OTHER: ....
....
....
....

INCLEMENT WEATHER PLAN:

....
....
....
....

CANCELLATION POLICY:

....
....
....
....

VENUE FIT

RATE EVERYTHING OUT OF 5

LOCATION:  TIME AVAILABLE:

OVERALL PRICE:  FOOD OPTIONS:

STAFF:  DRINK OPTIONS:

DECOR:  VIBE:

DATES AVAILABLE:

NOTES:

....
....
....
....
....

CATERING *Food*

Use this tool to help you select the right catering option for you.

CATERER: ....

CONTACT: ....

PHONE/EMAIL: ....

....

HOW MANY GUESTS DO YOU ANTICIPATE?

ADULTS: .... CHILDREN: .... VENDORS: ....

FOOD OPTIONS: DISHES YOU LIKE:

◯ Post Ceremony Canapes

....

....

◯ Post Dinner Canapes

....

....

◯ Entrees

....

....

◯ Mains

....

....

◯ Desserts

....

....

◯ Late Night Snacks

....

....

◯ Other

....

....

SERVING OPTIONS:

○ Alternating Drop		○ Set Menu
○ Buffet		○ Cocktail
○ A-la-carte		○ Banquet/Shared
○ Grazing		○ Food Trucks

SERVING OPTIONS:

○ Vegetarian		○ Gluten Free
○ Dairy Free		○ Allergies ....
○ Vegan		○ Other ....

CATERING NOTES:

....
....
....
....
....
....
....
....
....
....
....
....

CATERING *Beverages*

Use this tool to help you select the right catering option for you.

CATERER: ....

CONTACT: ....

PHONE/EMAIL: ....

....

....

HOW MANY GUESTS DO YOU ANTICIPATE?

ADULTS: .... CHILDREN: .... VENDORS: ....

OUR CHOICE OF DRINKS: LABELS YOU LIKE:

- ⚪ Light Beer
- ⚪ Full Strength Beer   ....
- ⚪ Craft Beer   ....
- ⚪ White Wine   ....
- ⚪ Red Wine   ....
- ⚪ Sparkling Wine   ....
- ⚪ Cocktails   ....
- ⚪ Spirits   ....
- ⚪ Signature Drinks   ....
- ⚪ Other   ....
- ⚪ Softdrink & Water   ....
- ⚪ Tea & Coffee   ....

ALL YOU NEED IS LOVE...

and Cake!

The size of your cake will be determined by the number of guests you wish to serve and what size portions you intend on serving. If you are already having desserts as part of your menu, you might like to serve finger sized pieces. Your venue is likely to charge a cake fee and that should include cutting it up and serving it with fresh cream.

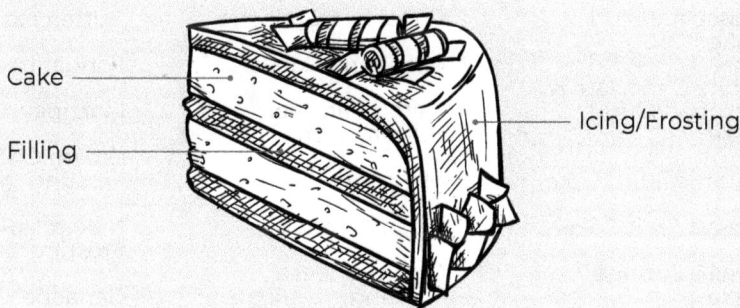

Cake ——————

Filling ——————

—————— Icing/Frosting

CAKE

Use this easy guide to help determine the size of cake you will need.

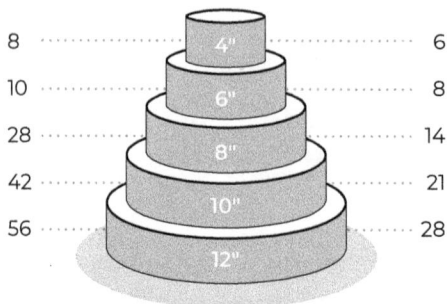

Finger size (1"x2")		Desert size (2"x2")
8	4"	6
10	6"	8
28	8"	14
42	10"	21
56	12"	28

ROUND CAKE

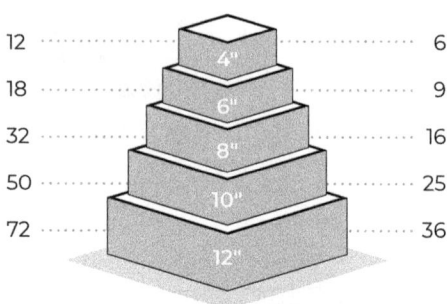

Finger size (1"x2")		Desert size (2"x2")
12	4"	6
18	6"	9
32	8"	16
50	10"	25
72	12"	36

SQUARE CAKE

The possibilities for your wedding cake are endless, but here are some of the most popular cake flavours to get you started.

CAKE:

- Chocolate Mud Cake
- White Chocolate & Raspberry Mud Cake
- Caramel Mud Cake
- Classic Fruit Cake
- Vanilla Sponge Cake
- Red Velvet Cake

FILLINGS:

- Chocolate Ganache
- Raspberry Coulis
- Salted Caramel Buttercream
- Marzipan
- Fresh Cream
- Cream Cheese Frosting

ICING/FROSTING:

- Buttercream
- Fondant
- Marzipan
- Cream Cheese Frosting
- Naked/No-Little Frosting
- Ganache

Now for the fun part! Test some cakes out and list your favourites.

CAKE: FILLINGS: ICING/FROSTING:

NOTES:

....

....

....

....

....

....

....

....

....

....

....

....

PHOTOGRAPHY

Make a list of the 'must have' photos you would like taken on the day.

Tip!

Take a photo of this list and give it to your photographer so you don't forget anything.

GETTING READY

....
....
....

THINGS AT HOME
(PETS, INVITATIONS, ETC.)

....
....
....

PRE-CEREMONY

....
....
....

CEREMONY

....
....
....
....

POST CEREMONY

....
....
....

BRIDAL PARTY

....
....
....

RECEPTION

....
....
....

OTHERS

....
....
....
....

FAMILY COMBINATIONS

....
....
....
....
....
....

FRIENDS COMBINATIONS

....
....
....
....
....

MUSIC

Tip!

Include an option to request a song on the RSVP cards to get your guests on the dance floor.

CEREMONY MUSIC

PROCESSIONAL (WEDDING PARTY) ....

PROCESSIONAL (FOR YOU) ....

SIGNING YOUR PAPERWORK ....

RECESSIONAL (AFTER CERMEONY) ....

OTHER ....

....

....

RECEPTION MUSIC

RECEPTION WELCOME SONG/S ....

FIRST DANCE ....

PARENT DANCE/S ....

CAKE CUTTING ....

GARTER TOSS ....

BOUQUET TOSS ....

EXIT SONG/S ....

'MUST PLAY' SONGS ....

....

'DO NOT PLAY' SONGS ....

....

OTHERS ....

....

....

FASHION

Make a list of the stores you would like to visit to find your dream outfits.

DRESS STORES TO TRY:

SUIT STORES TO TRY:

ACCESSORY STORES TO TRY:

SHOE STORES TO TRY:

NOTES:

Use this tool to keep track of your shortlisted items.

DRESS: ....
VEIL/HAIR PIECE: ....
SHOES: ....
UNDERWEAR: ....
JEWELLERY/ACCESSORIES: ....
OTHER: ....
....

SUIT: ....
CUFFLINKS: ....
TIES: ....
POCKET SQUARES: ....
JEWELLERY/ACCESSORIES: ....
SHOES: ....
OTHER: ....
....

MY BRIDAL PARTY OUTFITS: ....
SHOES: ....
JEWELLERY/ACCESSORIES: ....
OTHER: ....
....

FIANCÉ'S BRIDAL PARTY OUTFITS: ....
SHOES: ....
JEWELLERY/ACCESSORIES: ....
OTHER: ....
....

JUNIOR BRIDAL PARTY OUTFITS: ....
SHOES: ....
JEWELLERY/ACCESSORIES: ....
OTHER: ....

SIZING CHARTS

FEMALE

Bust (cm)	Waist (cm)	Hips (cm)	AUS	UK	USA	Europe
81	62	86	6	6	2	34
85	67	91	8	8	4	36
89	72	96	10	10	6	38
94	77	101	12	12	8	40
99	82	106	14	14	10	42
104	87	112	16	16	12	44
109	93	117	18	18	14	46
114	98	122	20	20	16	48
119	103	127	22	22	18	50
124	108	132	24	24	20	52
129	137	137	26	26	22	54

Our Measurements (cm)			
/	/	/	Measurements in centimetres

MALE	SMALL (cm)	MEDIUM (cm)	LARGE (cm)	EXTRA LARGE (cm)
Neck	37	39	42	44
Chest	91-98	99-106	107-113	114-121
Sleeve	84	86.5	89	91.5
Waist	73-80	81-88	89-96	97-103
Hip	86-93	94-101	102-108	109-116
Inseam	77.5	79	81	82.5
Our Measurements (cm)				
	/	/	/	/

Sizing refers to body measurements, not garment dimensions.

BRIDAL PARTY SIZING

NAME	DRESS SIZE	SHOE SIZE

NAME	PANT SIZE	SHIRT SIZE	SHOE SIZE

FLOWERS

If you are choosing fresh flowers, ask your local supplier to show you what flowers are in season and available at the time of your wedding. If you have 12 months or more until your day, you can get a good idea of what is available by looking around the same time of year as your wedding.

FLORAL ARRANGEMENTS: NOTES/PRICES:

Bride/s Bouquet

Grooms Buttonhole

Bridesmaid/s Bouquet

Maid of Honour Bouquet
(If different)

Groomsmen Buttonholes

Best Man Buttonhole
(If different)

Flowergirl/s Bouquet/
Buttonhole

Pageboy/s Buttonhole

Mothers of the Bride/Groom

Fathers of the Bride/Groom

Bouquet to Toss

Flowers for the Cake

Bridal Table

Centerpieces

Dog/Pet Collar

....

Arbour

....

Signs
(welcome, seating, etc.)

....

Bar

....

NOTES:

....
....
....
....
....
....
....
....
....
....
....
....
....
....
....
....
....
....
....
....

GIFTS

WEDDING GIFTS

If you have a preference for wedding gifts, don't forget to include it on your invitations.

OPTIONS: DETAILS:

○ Wishing Well   ....

○ Gift Registry   ....

○ No mention of gifts   ....

○ Other   ....

BONBONNIERE

List your favourite ideas for Bonbonniere.

ITEM: PRICE: QTY:

....

....

....

....

....

....

....

....

....

....

....

....

....

....

BRIDAL PARTY AND KEY ROLE GIFTS

Create a list of gifts you would like to give to thank your bridal party and key helpers/contributors.

NAME: GIFT IDEAS:

INVITATIONS

ARE YOU SENDING **SAVE THE DATE** CARDS?   Y   N

SEND BY: ....

INVITATIONS TO BE SENT BY: ....

RSVP REQUIRED BY: ....

INVITATION SIZES:

4.25 x 5.5" (107 x 139mm)

5 x 7" (117 x 182mm)

5.5 x 8.5" (139 x 216mm)

A5 (148 x 210mm)

A6 (105 x 148mm)

ENVELOPE SIZES:

C6 (114 x 162mm)

A7 (133 x 184mm)

C5 (162 x 229mm)

C5 (162 x 229mm)

C6 (114 x 162mm)

Save the date

Tip!

Check with the Post Office to find out how many stamps you will require for your envelopes. Having smaller envelopes can save on postage.

There are no rules when it comes to wording your invitations, but be sure to include the following details.

- Who's hosting
- The request to come to your wedding
- Your names
- Date and time
- The name and address of the ceremony and reception venues
- Dress code (if necessary)
- Separate RSVP card
- Information on gifts (if necessary)

LIST SOME IDEAS, THEMES AND WORDING FOR YOUR INVITATIONS:

....

....

....

....

....

....

....

....

....

....

....

Tip!

List the time of your ceremony a little earlier than you plan on your invitations. This will avoid having people arrive late.

THEME

Set the tone for your day with a theme or colour scheme.

WHICH STYLE DO YOU LIKE?

- Romanitc
- Alternative
- Modern
- Classic

- Bohemian
- Rustic
- Colourful
- No theme - Let's wing it!

THEME AND COLOUR SCHEME IDEAS:

....
....
....
....
....
....
....
....
....
....
....
....
....
....
....
....
....
....

STYLING IDEAS

NOTES

NOTES

Guests

The most
beautiful
thing to
hold on to is
each other

Guest List

**Stick to the basics, hold on to your family and friends -
they will never go out of fashion.**

Tip!

*We can almost guarantee that you will receive an RSVP or two
with no name on it. To save yourself the frustration, personalise
your RSVP cards OR discreetly write the corresponding number
on the back of their card.*

WEDDING GUESTLIST TRACKER

NAME OF GUEST	ADDRESS
1.	
2.	
3.	
4.	
5.	
6.	
7.	
8.	
9.	
10.	
11.	
12.	
13.	
14.	
15.	
16.	
17.	
18.	
19.	
20.	
21.	
22.	
23.	
24.	
25.	

RSVP	DIETARY REQUIREMENTS	TABLE NUMBER	GIFT RECEIVED

WEDDING GUESTLIST TRACKER

NAME OF GUEST	ADDRESS
26.	
27.	
28.	
29.	
30.	
31.	
32.	
33.	
34.	
35.	
36.	
37.	
38.	
39.	
40.	
41.	
42.	
43.	
44.	
45.	
46.	
47.	
48.	
49.	
50.	

RSVP	DIETARY REQUIREMENTS	TABLE NUMBER	GIFT RECEIVED

WEDDING GUESTLIST TRACKER

NAME OF GUEST	ADDRESS
51.	
52.	
53.	
54.	
55.	
56.	
57.	
58.	
59.	
60.	
61.	
62.	
63.	
64.	
65.	
66.	
67.	
68.	
69.	
70.	
71.	
72.	
73.	
74.	
75.	

RSVP	DIETARY REQUIREMENTS	TABLE NUMBER	GIFT RECEIVED

WEDDING GUESTLIST TRACKER

NAME OF GUEST	ADDRESS
76.	
77.	
78.	
79.	
80.	
81.	
82.	
83.	
84.	
85.	
86.	
87.	
88.	
89.	
90.	
91.	
92.	
93.	
94.	
95.	
96.	
97.	
98.	
99.	
100.	

RSVP	DIETARY REQUIREMENTS	TABLE NUMBER	GIFT RECEIVED

WEDDING GUESTLIST TRACKER

NAME OF GUEST	ADDRESS
101.	
102.	
103.	
104.	
105.	
106.	
107.	
108.	
109.	
110.	
111.	
112.	
113.	
114.	
115.	
116.	
117.	
118.	
119.	
120.	
121.	
122.	
123.	
124.	
125.	

RSVP	DIETARY REQUIREMENTS	TABLE NUMBER	GIFT RECEIVED

WEDDING GUESTLIST TRACKER

NAME OF GUEST	ADDRESS
126.	
127.	
128.	
129.	
130.	
131.	
132.	
133.	
134.	
135.	
136.	
137.	
138.	
139.	
140.	
141.	
142.	
143.	
144.	
145.	
146.	
147.	
148.	
149.	
150.	

RSVP	DIETARY REQUIREMENTS	TABLE NUMBER	GIFT RECEIVED

WEDDING GUESTLIST TRACKER

NAME OF GUEST	ADDRESS
151.	
152.	
153.	
154.	
155.	
156.	
157.	
158.	
159.	
160.	
161.	
162.	
163.	
164.	
165.	
166.	
167.	
168.	
169.	
170.	
171.	
172.	
173.	
174.	
175.	

RSVP	DIETARY REQUIREMENTS	TABLE NUMBER	GIFT RECEIVED

SEATING PLAN

TABLE #1

TABLE #3

TABLE #2

TABLE #4

TABLE #5

TABLE #7

TABLE #6

TABLE #8

SEATING PLAN

TABLE #9

....
....
....
....
....
....
....
....
....
....
....
....
....

TABLE #11

....
....
....
....
....
....
....
....
....
....
....
....
....

TABLE #10

....
....
....
....
....
....
....
....
....
....
....
....
....

TABLE #12

....
....
....
....
....
....
....
....
....
....
....
....
....

TABLE #13

....
....
....
....
....
....
....
....
....
....
....
....
....
....

TABLE #15

....
....
....
....
....
....
....
....
....
....
....
....
....
....

TABLE #14

....
....
....
....
....
....
....
....
....
....
....
....
....

TABLE #16

....
....
....
....
....
....
....
....
....
....
....
....
....

HENS PARTY/BRIDAL SHOWER

NAME OF GUEST	ADDRESS	DIETARY REQ.
1.		
2.		
3.		
4.		
5.		
6.		
7.		
8.		
9.		
10.		
11.		
12.		
13.		
14.		
15.		
16.		
17.		
18.		
19.		
20.		
21.		
22.		
23.		
24.		
25.		

NAME OF GUEST	ADDRESS	DIETARY REQ.
26.		
27.		
28.		
29.		
30.		
31.		
32.		
33.		
34.		
35.		
36.		
37.		
38.		
39.		
40.		
41.		
42.		
43.		
44.		
45.		
46.		
47.		
48.		
49.		
50.		

BUCKS PARTY

NAME OF GUEST	ADDRESS	DIETARY REQ.
1.		
2.		
3.		
4.		
5.		
6.		
7.		
8.		
9.		
10.		
11.		
12.		
13.		
14.		
15.		
16.		
17.		
18.		
19.		
20.		
21.		
22.		
23.		
24.		
25.		

NAME OF GUEST	ADDRESS	DIETARY REQ.
26.		
27.		
28.		
29.		
30.		
31.		
32.		
33.		
34.		
35.		
36.		
37.		
38.		
39.		
40.		
41.		
42.		
43.		
44.		
45.		
46.		
47.		
48.		
49.		
50.		

CHOOSING YOUR
Bridal Party

One of the hardest tasks is choosing your bridal party.
If you choose to have groomsmen and/or bridesmaids, set
aside some time to think about who you would like to have
take on this special role on your wedding day. Of course it will
be an honour for your bestie, sister, brother, cousin, etc to be
your bridesmaid or groomsman, but the role will also come
with some kind of responsibility and your expectation for
them to fulfil certain duties.

But how to choose?
If you're stuck, use the guide to help make your decision.

Tip!

*Don't forget to let them know up front if there will be any
expenses involved for taking this role. If you expect them to
pay for their outfits, hair & make up, let them know and set
a budget that works for everyone.*

SHOULD THIS PERSON BE IN OUR BRIDAL PARTY?

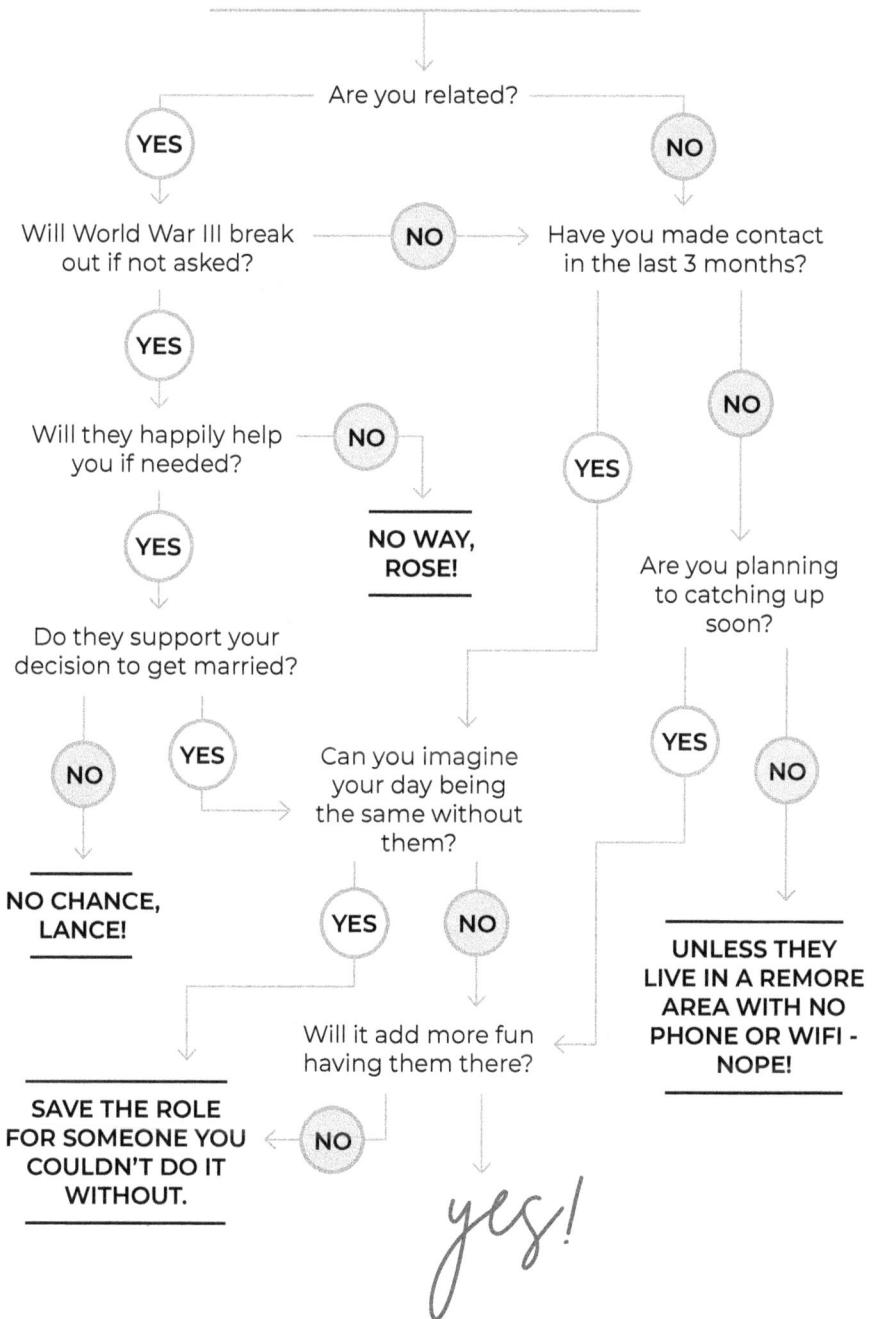

Are you related?

- **YES**
- **NO**

YES → Will World War III break out if not asked? **— NO →** Have you made contact in the last 3 months?

Will World War III break out if not asked?
- **YES →** Will they happily help you if needed?

Will they happily help you if needed?
- **NO →** NO WAY, ROSE!
- **YES →** Do they support your decision to get married?

Do they support your decision to get married?
- **NO →** NO CHANCE, LANCE!
- **YES →** Can you imagine your day being the same without them?

Have you made contact in the last 3 months?
- **YES →** Can you imagine your day being the same without them?
- **NO →** Are you planning to catching up soon?

Are you planning to catching up soon?
- **YES**
- **NO →** UNLESS THEY LIVE IN A REMORE AREA WITH NO PHONE OR WIFI - NOPE!

Can you imagine your day being the same without them?
- **YES**
- **NO →** Will it add more fun having them there?

Will it add more fun having them there?
- **NO →** SAVE THE ROLE FOR SOMEONE YOU COULDN'T DO IT WITHOUT.
- **yes!**

BRIDAL PARTY & OTHER ROLES

Make a list of all the people you would like to be in your bridal party and other key roles.

YOUR MAID OF HONOUR/BEST MAN

....

YOUR FIANCÉ'S BEST MAN/
MAID OF HONOUR

....

....

YOUR ATTENDANTS

....

....

....

FIANCÉ'S ATTENDANTS

....

....

....

JUNIOR ATTENDANTS

....

....

....

WITNESSES FOR CERTIFICATES

....

....

....

READERS

....

....

....

OTHER SPEAKERS

....

....

....

MC

....

ESCORT DOWN THE AISLE/
GIVE AWAY

....

PARENT DANCE

....

OTHER

....

....

Tip! *When asking your friends to be in your bridal party, be upfront about any costs and expectations to save any awkward chats about it later on.*

The Nitty Gritty

This is our
happily
ever after

WRITING YOUR VOWS

While there are no rules when it comes to writing your vows (apart from the legal bits), it's a good idea to make sure you and your Fiancé are on the same page in terms of length and style.

HOW DO YOU WANT YOUR CEREMONY TO FEEL?

- Serious
- Light-hearted
- Heartfelt
- Funny

- Romantic
- Religious
- Spiritual
- ....

HOW LONG DO YOU WANT YOUR WHOLE CEREMONY TO GO FOR?

- Bare minimum (legals only)
- Short and Sharp
- As long as necessary

NOTES:

....
....
....
....
....
....
....
....
....
....
....
....
....

Jot down your favourite memories, sayings, quotes, lyrics, poems, etc to help inspire you while writing your vows. You can ask your Celebrant to keep your vows a secret from each other so that you are sharing them for the first time on your wedding day of you like.

How did you and your Fiancé meet? What was your first impression?

....
....
....
....

What are the fun and unique things that makes your Fiancé them?

....
....
....
....

How did you know your Fiancé was 'the one'?

....
....
....
....

What are some of your funniest memories?

....
....
....
....

What are your Fiancé's biggest strengths?

....
....
....
....

WRITING YOUR VOWS

How does your Fiancé show that they love you?

....

....

....

What do you hope for the future? (e.g, children, travel, a new home)

....

....

....

What are your favourite things to do together?

....

....

....

What feelings do you get when you think about your future together?

....

....

....

What promises do you wish to make?

....

....

....

What does marriage mean to you?

....

....

....

List some of your favourite quotes, lyrics, poems or sayings.

WRITING YOUR VOWS

Let's get writing...

....
....
....
....
....
....
....
....
....
....
....
....
....
....
....
....
....
....
....
....
....
....
....
....
....
....

TRANSPORT

Make note of how you plan on getting yourselves and your guests (if necessary), around on the day of your wedding.

TO/FROM BEAUTY: ....

TO CEREMONY: ....

TO PHOTO LOCATION/S: ....

TO RECEPTION: ....

RETURN TO HOME/ACCOMMODATION: ....

TO HONEYMOON: ....

OTHER: ....

OTHER: ....

NOTES:

....
....
....
....
....
....
....
....
....
....
....
....
....
....
....
....

CEREMONY PLAN

LOCATION: ....

TIME: ....

OFFICIANT: ....

MUSIC: ....

DECORATIONS: ....

SIGNING TABLE: ....

SEATING FOR GUESTS: ....

FLOWERS: ....

SHADE/SHELTER: ....

NOTES:

....

....

....

....

....

....

....

....

....

....

....

....

....

....

....

CEREMONY

Get creative and sketch your ceremony setting.

POST-CEREMONY / GUESTS

If your ceremony and reception venues are the same, make sure your guests are comfortable while you're having your post-ceremony photos taken.

LOCATION: ....

TIME: ....

MUSIC: ....

SEATING: ....

SHADE/SHELTER: ....

FOOD/DRINKS: ....

NOTES:

....

....

....

....

....

....

....

....

....

....

....

....

....

....

....

....

RECEPTION PLANS

LOCATION: ....

TIME: ....

MUSIC: ....

PRE-DINNER DRINKS: ....

PRE-DINNER CANAPES: ....

TIME MEALS SERVED: ....

TIME OF SPEECHES: ....

CAKE CUTTING: ....

FIRST DANCE: ....

BOUQUET TOSS: ....

GARTER TOSS: ....

OTHER: ....

DECORATIONS REQUIRED: ....

....

NOTES:

....

....

....

....

....

....

....

....

....

Get creative and sketch your reception setting.

TRADITIONS

List any of your and your Fiancé's family customs or traditions that you might like to include.

MY FAMILY'S TRADITIONS:

....

....

....

....

....

....

....

....

....

....

....

....

....

....

....

....

....

....

....

....

....

....

....

FIANCÉ'S FAMILY'S TRADITIONS:

....

....

....

....

....

....

....

....

....

....

....

....

....

....

....

....

....

....

....

....

....

....

....

READERS, SPEECHES & TOASTS

Make a list of the people you would like to speak at your wedding and allocate time limits to avoid awkwardly long speeches.

CEREMONY SPEAKERS: DURATION: NOTES:

....

....

....

....

....

....

....

....

....

....

RECEPTION SPEECHES   DURATION: NOTES:
& TOASTS:

....

....

....

....

....

....

....

....

....

....

....

....

REHEARSAL

Make a plan for what you want to achieve at your rehearsal and the people you require to attend.

DATE: ....

LOCATION: ....

TIME: ....

PEOPLE REQUIRED TO ATTEND: NOTES:

TASKS TO COMPLETE:

ALLOCATED TO:

REHEARSAL

Officiant

Bridesmaids   Maid of Honour   Best Man   Groomsmen

Flower Girl   Bride & Groom   Page Boy

PRE-CEREMONY NOTES:

....

....

....

....

....

....

MUSIC/SONGS:

	NOTES:

....

....

....

....

....

....

....

....

....

....

ENTRANCE ORDER:

....

....

....

....

....

....

....

....

....

....

....

NOTES:

....

....

....

....

....

....

....

....

....

....

....

KEY ROLES: (PRAYER, READING, ETC)

....

....

....

....

....

....

....

....

....

....

....

....

....

NOTES:

....

....

....

....

....

....

....

....

....

....

....

....

....

REHEARSAL

EXIT ORDER:

NOTES:

NOTES:

VIP CONTACTS

Contact
Phone   Email

Contact
Phone   Email

Contact
Phone   Email

Contact
Phone   Email

Contact
Phone   Email

Contact
Phone   Email

Contact
Phone   Email

Contact
Phone   Email

Contact
Phone   Email

Contact
Phone   Email

Contact
Phone   Email

Contact
Phone   Email

Contact
Phone   Email

Contact
Phone   Email

Contact
Phone   Email

Contact
Phone   Email

Contact
Phone   Email

WEDDING DAY

Things to take

Make a list of everything you, your fiancé and your bridal party need to take on the day.

Rings

Dresses

Shoes

Veil/Hair Accessories

Perfume/Cologne

Make Up and Hairspray

Suits/Shirts/Ties

Appropriate Socks

Cufflinks/Accessories/Belts

Deodorant

Vows and Speeches

....

....

....

Accidents happen!

Be prepared to any kind of wardrobe malfunction, blisters or zits by putting together a little emergency kit.

Bobby Pins

Sanitary Items

Cotton Tips

Double-Sided Tape

Needle and Thread

Safety Pins

Pain Killers

Comb

Glue

Mints

Floss

Bandaids

WEDDING DAY *Schedule*

6:00am	3:00pm
6:30am	3:30pm
7:00am	4:00pm
7:30am	4:30pm
8:00am	5:00pm
8:30am	5:30pm
9:00am	6:00pm
9:30am	6:30pm
10:00am	7:00pm
10:30am	7:30pm
11:00am	8:00pm
11:30am	8:30pm
12:00pm	9:00pm
12:30pm	9:30pm
1:00pm	10:00pm
1:30pm	10:30pm
2:00pm	11:00pm
2:30pm	11:30pm

WEDDING DAY *schedule for MC*

Time	
3:00pm	
3:30pm	
4:00pm	
4:30pm	
5:00pm	
5:30pm	
6:00pm	
6:30pm	
7:00pm	
7:30pm	
8:00pm	
8:30pm	
9:00pm	
9:30pm	
10:00pm	
10:30pm	
11:00pm	
11:30pm	

NOTES

....
....
....
....
....
....
....
....
....
....
....
....
....
....
....
....
....
....
....
....
....
....
....
....
....
....
....

WEDDING DAY *getting ready*

MAKEUP ARTIST #1:
....

CONTACT: ....

PRICE PER PERSON: ....
TIME PER PERSON: ....
TIME: NAME:
....
....
....
....
....
....
....
....

MAKEUP ARTIST #2:
....

CONTACT: ....

PRICE PER PERSON: ....
TIME PER PERSON: ....
TIME: NAME:
....
....
....
....
....
....
....
....

HAIRDRESSER #1:
....

CONTACT: ....

PRICE PER PERSON: ....
TIME PER PERSON: ....
TIME: NAME:
....
....
....
....
....
....
....
....

HAIRDRESSER #2:
....

CONTACT: ....

PRICE PER PERSON: ....
TIME PER PERSON: ....
TIME: NAME:
....
....
....
....
....
....
....
....

PACK DOWN

Make a list of all the items that need to be packed up to go home or be returned to hire companies. This is very useful if you won't be there to pack things up or if you have people helping you.

ITEM	QTY	RETURN TO	WHEN

HONEYMOON

DESTINATION: ....

DATE: ....

TRAVEL TIMES: ....

HOW WE ARE GETTING THERE: ....
....

TRAVEL DOCUMENTS REQUIRED: ....
....

TRAVEL REFERENCE/FLIGHT #: ....

THINGS TO DO AND SEE: ....
....
....
....
....
....
....
....
....
....
....

RETURN DATE: ....

TRAVEL TIMES: ....

TRAVEL REFERENCE/FLIGHT #: ....

NOTES: ....
....
....
....
....
....
....

HONEYMOON

DATES BOOKED: ....
HOTEL NAME: ....
ADDRESS: ....
....
PHONE: ....
REFEERENCE NUMBER: ....
NOTES: ....
....
....
....
....
....
....
....

DATES BOOKED: ....
HOTEL NAME: ....
ADDRESS: ....
....
PHONE: ....
REFEERENCE NUMBER: ....
NOTES: ....
....
....
....
....
....
....
....

DATES BOOKED: ....

HOTEL NAME: ....

ADDRESS: ....

....

PHONE: ....

REFEERENCE NUMBER: ....

NOTES: •..

....

....

....

....

....

....

....

....

DATES BOOKED: ....

HOTEL NAME: ....

ADDRESS: ....

....

PHONE: ....

REFEERENCE NUMBER: ....

NOTES: ....

....

....

....

....

....

....

....

IVORY HAUS
—— EST. 2016 ——

WWW.**IVORYHAUS**.COM.AU
WWW.FACEBOOK.COM/**LOVEIVORYHAUS**
HELLO@IVORYHAUS.COM.AU
WWW.INSTAGRAM.COM/**IVORY.HAUS**